THE UNITED ARAB EMIRATES

U.A.E.

JULIA JOHNSON

ACKNOWLEDGEMENTS

The Author and Publishers are grateful to the following organizations and individuals for permission to reproduce copyright illustrations in this book:

Embassy of the United Arab Emirates, London; Hutchison Photo Library; Ministry of Information of the United Arab Emirates; Norman D. Price/Vidocq Photo Library; Helene Rogers; Frank Spooner Pictures.

Published by Chelsea House Publishers

Printed and bound in Hong Kong

First printing

ISBN 1–55546–178–6

Chelsea House Publishers

Harold Steinberg, Chairman & Publisher
Susan Lusk, Vice President
A Division of Chelsea House Educational Communications, Inc.

133 Christopher Street, New York, NY 10014

345 Whitney Avenue, New Haven, CT 05510

5014 West Chester Pike, Edgemont, PA 19028

Contents

ARABIAN GU

QATAR

DAS ISLAND

Jebel Dhanna

Ruwais

ABU

SAUDI ARABIA

IRAQ

KUWAIT

IRAN

ARABIAN GULF

QATAR

SAUDI
ARABIA

OMAN

LIWA C

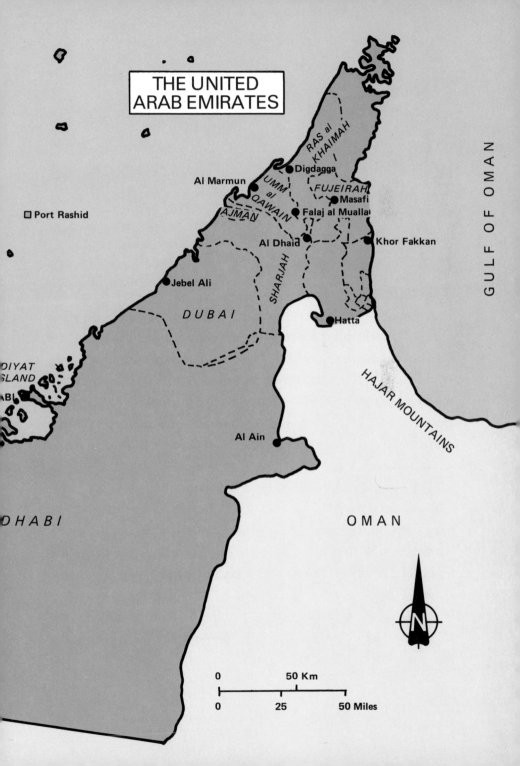

A Land of Contrasts and Surprises

The United Arab Emirates: the name might conjure up the traditional image of Arabs riding through the sands on their camels. Since the discovery of petroleum, which has put the country on the map, most people would also include a backdrop of oil rigs. There certainly is sand—lots of it—and camels—many of them—and oil—plenty of it. But there is much more besides. The UAE is a land of contrasts and surprises, of old and new living in harmony side by side, and most of all it is a land of welcome.

The United Arab Emirates, a federation of seven Emirates, came into being in December 1971. Before independence, the area was under British control through a series of treaty arrangements dating back to 1820. From one of them, the General Treaty on Maritime Truce, the area received the name "The Trucial States".

Lying on the south-east corner of the Arabian peninsula, the UAE enjoys the longest coast on the Arabian Gulf, extending

Traditional *dhows* (cargo ships) and modern buildings side by side in Dubai

approximately six hundred kilometres (over 370 miles) in the north and one hundred kilometres (over sixty miles) on the Arabian Sea in the east. Excluding the islands, it covers an area of about 77,000 square kilometres (30,000 square miles). From east to west the Emirates are Abu Dhabi, Dubai, Sharjah, Ajman, Umm al Qawain, Ras al Khaimah and Fujeirah. Six of them lie on the coast of the Arabian Gulf while the seventh, Fujeirah, is situated on the eastern coast of the peninsula and

9

Boats moored in the harbour at Khor Fakkan. The mountains in the background are in neighbouring Oman

has direct access to the Gulf of Oman in the Indian Ocean. This is an area of very shallow seas, offshore islands and coral reefs. The UAE is geologically a stable zone and there is little likelihood of major earthquakes or volcanic eruptions.

Qatar lies to the west of the UAE, and Oman to the east. The UAE also has a large boundary with Saudi Arabia on the northern fringes of the Rub al Khali, or Empty Quarter. Abu Dhabi is the largest Emirate, with an area of over 65,000 square kilometres (25,000 square miles). Abu Dhabi town is also the capital of the UAE. It lies on a triangular island, linked to the mainland by two bridges. The ruler of Abu Dhabi, H. H. Sheikh Zayed bin Sultan al Nahyan, is the country's President. The most important port is Dubai because of its

10

position on one of the rare deep creeks of the area. H. H. Sheikh Rashid bin Said al Maktoum, ruler of Dubai, is the country's Vice-President and, since April 1979, he has also been the Prime Minister. Sheikh Zayed and Sheikh Rashid, together with the rulers of the other five Emirates, make up the Supreme Council of Rulers of the Federal Government.

The UAE is classed as a desert because it receives less than 25 centimetres (10 inches) of rain a year. One-eighth of the world is desert, and the largest, hottest deserts are in the Arab world.

Some plant life has adapted to desert conditions. Seeds, protected by tough coverings, can be blown around for years waiting for moisture or a suitable spot to germinate. Some plants have few leaves so that little water is lost to the air. Some have developed spines to stop animals eating them. Others, known as succulents, have fleshy stems in which water is stored. Still others grow very long roots to penetrate the soil down to the water table. The roots of the mesquite, for example, can grow over thirty-five metres (115 feet) long and those of the tamarisk over fifty metres (164 feet).

Soils in the UAE are generally coarse and sandy and contain little organic matter. *Sabkah* is the name for the salty mud-flats which run the length of the coastline. With the exception of the oases, most of the Emirates are so arid that sustained agriculture is not possible without artificial irrigation. Some protection against high winds and high summer temperatures is also necessary. An oasis is a fertile spot where water is more abundant and settled agriculture is possible. The largest oases are to be

11

Sheikh Zayed bin Sultan al Nahyan (*second from left*) and Sheikh Rashid bin Said al Maktoum (*centre*) at the opening of the UAE earth satellite station

found in the Emirate of Abu Dhabi. Al Ain is the most fertile and extensive oasis, whilst the Liwa is a string of small oases on the edge of the Rub al Khali. The Liwa was a regular and vital stopping point for caravans crossing the desert. Lush greenery is also to be found at Al Dhaid oasis in the Emirate of Sharjah, at Hatta in Dubai, and at the agricultural centre of Umm al Qawain at Falaj al Mualla oasis. Ras al Khaimah, the most northerly of the Emirates, is the most fertile of them all.

12

Most of the UAE is flat, but to the east the barren, rugged Hajar mountains divide the country into the Dhahira, or Gulf coast, and the Batinah coast on the Indian Ocean. The mountains are full of steep-sided valleys known as *wadis*. When rain falls, it can come in a sudden localized downpour and can cause flash floods. Sudden torrents carry away soil from the dried-up *wadis* and make them even deeper. There are no permanent rivers in the Gulf and only a few short streams in the mountains.

Much of the land is covered with sand. Often, sand is blown into dunes. Sand dunes are a dominant feature of the landscape. Crescent-shaped sand dunes, called *barchans* (pronounced "bar-kaans"), are formed by the wind blowing in one direction. Strong winds and sandstorms are common. June usually sees the onset of seasonal north-westerly winds over most of the Gulf area, known generally as the "forty-day *shamal*". At this time of the year, the climate seems choking and oppressive. Localized eddies swirl dust and leaves and paper about. In the central Gulf area, the summer *shamal* blows with varying strength. It can occasionally reach gale force with rough seas. Sometimes a thick dust haze blows from the dust bowl in Iraq.

From October to mid-May, the weather is ideal with clear, warm sunny days and pleasantly cool nights. Fog can occur at night, especially on the coast. From May onwards the temperature rises steadily. The average temperature in July and August is around 40 degrees Celsius (105 degrees Fahrenheit), but it can reach as high as 48 degrees Celsius (118 degrees

13

Desert flowers. Despite the arid and harsh environment of much of the UAE, some plants and animals are able to survive

Fahrenheit). This, combined with a high level of humidity, makes for a very uncomfortable summer. From June to August, humidity levels average ninety-seven per cent. In such conditions, strenuous outdoor activity can be dangerous. However, houses, shops and offices, and even cars, are almost always fully air-conditioned. The summer climate is too hot even for people who like sun-bathing.

One world record which the Gulf can claim is that of the highest sea surface temperatures. In the central and eastern Gulf, summer sea temperatures reach 34-35 degrees Celsius (93-95 degrees Fahrenheit). The highest temperature recorded to date is 36 degrees Celsius (96.8 degrees Fahrenheit). In lagoons, the temperature can exceed 40 degrees Celsius (104 degrees

Fahrenheit) which makes swimming extremely uncomfortable. A dip in the sea ceases to be refreshing when the sea temperature is higher than skin temperature.

It is estimated that the total UAE national population is between 250,000 and 300,000. The official language is Arabic, although English is widely spoken. All the native inhabitants are Muslim, mainly of the Sunni sect. (The Sunni are one of two sects to emerge after the death of the Prophet Muhammad due to a difference of opinion over who should be Muhammad's successor. The other sect are called Shi'ite Muslims.) With their background of navigation and exploration, the ancestors of the Arabs of the Emirates can be traced back to many parts of the world, from Aden to Zanzibar. Skin colour in the Emirates varies from light brown to black, and facial characteristics are

Barchans — crescent-shaped sand dunes formed by the wind blowing consistently in one direction

equally varied. This cosmopolitan heritage leads to a cosmopolitan outlook.

There are also many non-Arab immigrant workers. In the coastal towns there are many Iranians, Indians, Pakistanis, Baluchis and Blacks—the latter being descended from slaves who were transported from Africa during the course of several centuries of slave trading. Other expatriates, including Westerners, make up about 5.5 per cent of the total population.

The UAE has developed at an amazing pace. Progress in education and health facilities, for example, has been dramatic. The country was fortunate to be blessed with large quantities of oil, and revenue from oil dominates the economy. Between 1971 and 1980, the UAE's revenue from petroleum grew about twenty-five-fold, and the economy expanded very rapidly—particularly between 1973 and 1976.

The UAE belongs to both the thirteen-member Organization of Petroleum Exporting Countries (OPEC) and the nine-member Organization of Arab Petroleum Exporting Countries (OAPEC). Oil production reached its peak in 1977. During recent years, production has been generally falling off as a result of a deliberate policy of consolidating resources, and because of OPEC production cutback. Although the UAE is capable of producing about three million barrels of oil a day, it is currently producing 1.1 million barrels a day.

It is due to the far-sightedness of its rulers that the UAE has achieved so much in so short a time but underlying this progress is the firm foundation of Islam.

16

Digging into the Past

Archaeological findings show that there was an advanced civilization in the coastal area of what is now the UAE as long ago as the third millenium B.C. The community traded with the inhabitants of the Indus Valley in Pakistan to the east, and of Mesopotamia to the west. The Gulf has always been a waterway for trade. Assyrian and Babylonian merchants once passed this way, with cargoes of frankincense, spices, pearls, metals and timbers. A Mesopotamian clay tablet speaks of "fishes' eyes". These are the pearls for which the Gulf was famed for the next three thousand years. The lives of the Gulf peoples have always centred around the sea. Their *dhows*—great seafaring ships—have changed little in construction over the centuries. The craft of *dhow*-building continues today on the beaches of Ajman.

In ancient times the region had a very different climate. There was more rain, which meant that it was easier to grow crops. This encouraged communities to settle. Major excavations at

Hili, near Al Ain, have unearthed seeds and stalks of wheat, barley, oats and sorghum, as well as date stones and melon seeds. These show that a settled pastoral community inhabited the area in about 3000 B.C. The presence of fossils in the dunes also indicates that the shoreline was once considerably further inland.

Tombs have also been unearthed, along with a copper smelting site, a well and irrigation or drainage channels. One large, beehive-shaped stone structure, with relief carvings, has been restored, and can be seen today in the Hili Gardens public park. Pottery and soapstone vessels were found in the tombs, along with cornelian (a reddish-yellow semi-precious stone) and shell beads, and copper and bronze arrowheads.

Another major settlement and tomb site, dating from

***Dhows,* the traditional ships of the Gulf, have changed little in design and are still built on the beaches of the Emirate of Ajman as they have been for very many centuries**

A tomb at Hili, near Al Ain, dating from about 3000 B.C.

approximately 2700 B.C., is at Umm al Nar, near Abu Dhabi. This was unearthed in the mid-1950s, and was the first archaeological site to be discovered in the area. Engravings on a tomb here include pictures of camels. Camels and donkeys were probably familiar animals at this time. It is generally accepted that the camel became domesticated during the third millenium B.C. Artefacts found at these sites suggest that the population engaged in fishing, weaving and wheat-growing. They also show that the inhabitants had connections with other sites across the Gulf—for example, Tepe Yahya in Iran and the

Indus Valley in Pakistan. Main exports from the UAE were soapstone vessels and copper. Evidence suggests that the peninsula—northern Oman and the UAE—was the copper-producing country known as Magan, which is mentioned in old Mesopotamian inscriptions.

Excavations in Ras al Khaimah Emirate have revealed that the ancient palace of the legendary Queen of Sheba was probably in the village of Shimal. Many tombs dating from the second millenium B.C. stretch along the foot of the hills in this area. Evidence of trade with other regions persists: in the tombs were a broken jar from Harappa in the Indus Valley (Pakistan) and a cube-shaped weight from the same area.

Between 900 and 500 B.C., the Qusais area of Dubai was the centre of an Iron Age town. In 1979, the first complete Iron Age skeleton to be found in the Lower Gulf was unearthed. Pots buried along with the body suggest that the people of the time believed in life after death. During the Iron Age, a network of land trade routes crossed the country, and agriculture developed in oasis settlements with the spread of a system of irrigation channels known as *falaj*.

In the seventh century A.D., Islam swept through the Arabian peninsula. A trading post of the early Islamic era has been discovered in Jumeirah, which is now a fashionable residential area of Dubai. The trading post seems to have been at its height during the fifth or sixth century A.D. The settlement includes houses, a governor's residence, a marketplace, and a hunting-lodge with snares for trapping wild animals, probably foxes.

The first complete Iron Age skeleton to be unearthed in the Lower Gulf area

Many ancient fortifications can still be found all over the Emirates. Watchtowers guarding mountain passes suggest a history of raiding.

Investigation into archaeological sites is encouraged both by the UAE government and by individual Emirates. There is a Council of Cultural Heritage, as well as a Centre for Documentation and Research. Large-scale restoration is being carried out on old buildings. For example, the historical Old Fort Palace in Abu Dhabi, built about two hundred years ago, and the house of Sheikh Rashid's father, in Dubai, are being preserved.

21

The Old Fort Palace in Abu Dhabi, built about two hundred years ago and now restored to its former glory

Key discoveries from archaeological sites are displayed in the country's two museums, in Al Ain and Dubai. Another museum is being set up in Ras al Khaimah. Dubai Museum is housed in the Al Fihaidi fort, which is itself an historic building. It is considered to be the oldest building in the Emirate of Dubai and was built in about 1800. The walls were constructed of coral and shell rubble collected from the sea, cemented together with lime. Before being opened as a museum, it was part of Dubai's defences against the attacks of neighbouring tribes. Later, it became the ruler's residence and the seat of government, as well as a jail and an ammunition store.

22

From Foreign Rule to Independence

In the fifteenth century, the Portuguese seized control of shipping on both sides of the Indian Ocean. By the early sixteenth century, they had gained control of the Gulf. They took over trade from Arab and Indian merchants, shipping goods from the Far East. A garrison and customs house were set up at Julfar, now Ras al Khaimah. In 1517, the Portuguese writer Durate Barbosa wrote a description of Julfar: "There dwell persons of worth, great navigators and wholesale dealers. Here is a very great fishery as well of seed pearls as of large pearls, and the Moors of Hormuz come hither to buy them and carry them to India and many other lands."

The Portuguese were the first Europeans in the Gulf for many centuries. They were the scourge of Gulf seafarers, as they were cruel, and subjected their prisoners to torture and degradation. Their occupation was bitterly resisted by the two main tribal forces, the Bani Yas and the Al Qawasim.

By the end of the sixteenth century, Holland and Britain were

23

also trying to establish trade in the Gulf. Portuguese supremacy gradually declined and, in 1650, the Portuguese were compelled to withdraw. There followed a period of rivalry between the Dutch and the British. Initially, the Dutch were dominant. British fortunes improved with the establishment of the British East India Company and, in 1766, the Dutch lost power.

Piracy was common in the Gulf during the seventeenth and eighteenth centuries, and reached its height at the beginning of the nineteenth century. From the mid-eighteenth century onwards, the strongest tribe in the Gulf was the Qawasim of Ras al Khaimah. They ruled their territorial waters, demanding a toll from ships passing through. They earned a reputation as pirates, and the coastline became known as the "Pirate Coast". "Pirates", however, was the name given to them by the British. It is often felt today that this was an unfair description of the Qawasim in their struggles against the British East India Company.

Attacks on British ships led to British expeditions against the pirates. In 1805, the British government in India sent a force to the Gulf. As a result the first treaty between the coastal tribes and the British was signed. However, this did not suppress the Qawasim. Further expeditions followed in 1809, 1811 and 1818. In 1820, the British destroyed the main Qawasim fleet at Ras al Khaimah and then signed a general treaty of peace with the Qawasim and all the sheikhs of the coast. A strong British squadron was stationed at Ras al Khaimah. In addition, a local Political Agent based at Sharjah was appointed to represent the

British and to see that the sheikhs held to the signed treaty.

While the Qawasim controlled the coastal areas, the Bani Yas were the most powerful tribe in the interior. Late in the eighteenth century, numbers of them settled in the coastal areas of Abu Dhabi and Dubai. In 1835, they signed a truce to refrain from tribal quarrels during the all-important summer pearling season.

In 1853, the British signed a perpetual maritime treaty with the rulers of the coastal tribes and undertook to protect the states from outside attack. The coast became known as the Trucial Coast, or Trucial Oman.

Ties with Britain were further strengthened in 1892 when the sheikhs signed an ''exclusive agreement'', preventing them from dealing with the government of any foreign power other than Britain. This meant, for instance, that in 1911 the Political Agent was entitled to ask the rulers not to grant concessions to a Greek merchant who wanted to fish for pearls and sponges in the Gulf. Again, in the 1920s and 1930s the rulers were asked not to allow any foreigners to enjoy concessions for banking or oil without British approval.

In 1951, the British established a military force known as the Trucial Oman Scouts, to keep order and to help with oil exploration in the interior. Also in 1951, a Trucial Council was established. The seven rulers met at least twice a year under the chairmanship of the British Political Agent in Dubai.

Oil was discovered in commercial quantities in 1958 in Abu Dhabi Emirate. The first shipment followed in 1962. With the granting of concessions to drill for oil, it became essential to define the borders between the states. As the UAE became one of the richest nations on earth, rapid development followed. Britain had previously played a peace-keeping role; now it became active in encouraging development.

In 1968, Britain announced its intention of withdrawing from the Gulf in 1971. In the same year, Sheikh Zayed of Abu Dhabi and Sheikh Rashid of Dubai met at Al Smaih on the border between their two Emirates. They agreed to unite the two Emirates in a single federation, which the neighbouring states were also invited to join. Meetings were held with the rulers

A parade celebrating UAE National Day. The UAE became an independent state in 1971 following Britain's withdrawal from the area

of all the present UAE states, and with those of Bahrain and Qatar, who subsequently chose to remain independent.

On December 2, 1971, the UAE became a sovereign, independent, federal state. Initially, there were six member states as Ras al Khaimah did not join the federation until February 1972. All previous treaties with Britain were replaced with a Treaty of Friendship. Membership of the Arab League and the United Nations followed. Some years later, the Gulf States Co-operation Council was established.

Towards an Understanding of the UAE

The people of the UAE are Muslims—followers of Islam. The word *Islam* means "submission". The religion of Islam is the main foundation of the customs and traditions of the Gulf region. To understand the people of the UAE or, for that matter, the people of the Islamic world in general, one has to first have some understanding of their religion.

Islam cannot be separated from everyday life. It is a total way of life. A Muslim believes that if he lives in accordance with the teachings of the Holy Quran he will attain after-life in Paradise. The Quran is the Muslim holy book, and it provides a complete guide for life. Nothing is left out. There is guidance on marriage, divorce, bringing up children, inheritance, justice and even business conduct.

The Quran is God's word revealed to the Prophet Muhammad by the Angel Gabriel. Muhammad was born in A.D. 570 in Mecca in Saudi Arabia. He was over forty when he started receiving messages from God. At first he was doubtful

28

and afraid, but eventually he began to preach. Paganism and corruption were widespread at this time. In A.D.622, the authorities forced Muhammad and his followers to leave Mecca. They decided to go to Medina. This is known as the Hejira which means "flight" or "departure" in Arabic. (To Muslims this took place on the first day of year 1—they calculate all dates from this day, just as Christians calculate dates from the birth of Jesus.) The people of Medina immediately followed Muhammad. There were many battles between the people of Mecca and the people of Medina. Eventually, Muhammad and his followers were victorious at Badr in A.D.630.

The Islamic religion spread quickly. It reached the UAE during the Prophet's lifetime in the middle of the seventh century. The last great battle of Islam, which established the Muslim religion in Arabia for ever, was fought in A.D.630, near Dibba in the UAE. By A.D.732, Muslim armies had conquered the whole of the Middle East and North Africa.

A Muslim believes in one God who is called Allah. Allah is the same God who is worshipped by Jews and Christians. Muslims also believe in Jesus, but they believe that Jesus was the last of the prophets before Muhammad. Belief in Allah is one of the Five Pillars of Islam, and a Muslim affirms this belief with the statement: "There is no God but Allah, and Muhammad is his Prophet". The other four are prayer, fasting, pilgrimage and giving alms to the poor.

Five times a day, at dawn, noon, afternoon, dusk and after dark, a Muslim must stop whatever he is doing to pray. He

Muslims at prayer facing the holy city of Mecca

prays facing towards the holy city of Mecca, kneeling and
touching the ground with his forehead in submission to Allah.

Whenever possible, he must try to go to the mosque to pray.
The mosque is the Muslim place of worship. Only men go into
the mosques; the women usually pray at home. Some mosques
are very simple, whilst others are extremely elaborate. Every
mosque has a tower called a minaret. In the past, a man known
as a *muezzin* would call the faithful to prayer from the top of
the minaret. Nowadays, loudspeakers relay his call.

There are more than 1,500 mosques throughout the UAE—an
indication of a living and vibrant faith. Outside each mosque
there is a fountain or running water, so that people may wash
before praying. Before entering the mosque a Muslim must also
take off his shoes.

30

The holy day of the Muslim week is Friday. The weekend starts on Thursday afternoon, and people go back to work on Saturday. On Fridays, the Imam, or spiritual leader, reads from the Quran and preaches a sermon.

Ramadan is the ninth month of the Muslim year. Islam follows a lunar calendar, and so the month of Ramadan falls at a different time each year. Ramadan commemorates the month during which the Quran was first revealed to the Prophet

The slender minaret of a mosque in Sharjah. Nowadays the *muezzin*'s call is relayed by loudspeaker

Muhammad. It starts with the first sighting of the moon. It is traditional for groups of children to call on neighbours after dark, and be treated to Ramadan nuts and sweets. They carry lanterns called *fanoos*.

During Ramadan, a Muslim is required to fast from dawn to dusk. This does not include children. Anyone who is ill or on a journey is not expected to fast, but should make up the missed time later. It is thought that the self-denial and discipline involved in fasting nourish the soul. Fasting can be particularly difficult when Ramadan falls during the very hot summer months. In Ramadan non-Muslims are expected to respect Islamic rites and should not eat, drink or smoke in public during daylight hours.

In the UAE, and in many other Muslim countries, the beginning and end of the daily fast is announced by the firing of a cannon. *Imsak* is the name of the meal before dawn, and *iftar* the meal after dusk. In some places a *musahir* also wanders the streets to wake people up for the *imsak* meal. He sings songs and beats his drum.

In the evening, after the day-long fasting and prayer, the streets come to life. Fruit-merchants and sherbet-vendors sell their wares, and many food stalls are set up on street corners. Traditionally, the fast is broken by a simple meal of dates and curd. There follows a substantial meal, which the women have probably spent much of the day preparing.

Ramadan ends at the sighting of the new moon. It is celebrated by the feast of Eid al Fitr. At dawn the men and boys

Firing a cannon to announce the end of the daily fast during Ramadan

gather in the mosques to pray. Then they visit the Sheikh to offer greetings. *Eid Mubarak* (''May your Eid be blessed'') is the customary greeting.

The *musahir* usually visits the people he has helped to wake up for the *imsak* meal. They give him Eid sweets and money to thank him for his efforts during Ramadan. The children are also given presents. The women pay their respects to the Sheikha, the wife of the Sheikh. They visit one another and eat sweets and drink coffee. It is customary to wash in rosewater, and to inhale fragrant incense.

Every Muslim who can possibly manage it must make the pilgrimage to Mecca at least once in his lifetime. This is called the *Hajj* and the pilgrim is called the *hajji*. The pilgrimage to

33

Mecca dates back to ancient times. Muhammad included it in the religion of Islam to encourage peace between Mecca and Medina. The pilgrim enters the courtyard of the Great Mosque at Mecca wearing a white, seamless garment. He walks seven times round the Kaa'ba, a large rectangular building containing a sacred black stone, which the pilgrim kisses. The Quran says that the Kaa'ba was built by Ibrahim (Abraham) and his son Ismail to house the stone, which was given to them by the Angel Gabriel. Some say that the stone is a meteorite. The end of the *Hajj* is celebrated by the Eid al Adha, or Feast of Sacrifice.

The fifth Pillar of Islam, giving alms to the poor, is called *zakat*. Each Muslim surrenders 2.5 per cent of his wealth and property in order to help those less fortunate than himself. There is no begging in the UAE, since an extensive state financial aid system supports any national who cannot support himself.

The written language of the Quran is a unifying link between Muslims throughout the world. Although spoken Arabic has changed over the centuries and varies from country to country, the written word has not. Arabs today still write the same Arabic as they wrote over one thousand years ago. The same cannot be said of the English language—the language of Chaucer, and even of Shakespeare, is difficult for us to understand today. But Arabic is very much a living language. It is written from right to left and the script is very beautiful. In fact, it is often used as an art form, since the Quran says that it is wrong to make pictures or statues of living things.

The Quran is also the major source of Islamic law, which

34

is known as *Sharia*. Islamic law is also based on the *hadiths*, or sayings, of the Prophet Muhammad. In Sharia law, the plaintiff and defendant sit side by side before the court. Evidence on oath is acceptable since a Muslim believes that he will be eternally damned on a false oath. He would far rather take punishment under the law than risk the fires of hell. The crime rate in the UAE is low.

Islamic law allows a man to have up to four wives at the same time. The Prophet Muhammad allowed polygamy because of the number of men killed in battle in his day. Polygamy was one way of protecting widows and orphans. However, the Quran requires that all wives should be treated equally. Nowadays, polygamy is becoming less common.

Lifestyles and Traditions

Great importance is attached to hospitality in the UAE, as it is in all countries of the Middle East. It is considered an honour both to invite and to be invited into a home for a meal. When preparing food it is common to allow for an unexpected guest. There is an Arabic saying which goes: "If there is not more than enough, there is not enough." In the past, if a Bedouin came across a stranger in the desert it would be a matter of honour to take him home for a feast. The ultimate in traditional hospitality is to slaughter a sheep or goat for the guest. An animal killed for food must have its throat cut "in the name of Allah, Allah is most great". A woman may not slaughter, though she may guide the hand of her son if no man is available.

Cooking ability is rated highly among feminine accomplishments. A meal often begins with a variety of savoury appetizers known as *mezze*. *Houmous* is a puree of chick peas mixed with olive oil, lemon, garlic and *tahini* (a paste made from sesame seeds). (Garlic is thought to have healing properties and

36

to ward off the evil eye.) *Tabbouleh* is a dish made from cracked wheat, parsley, tomato, mint, lemon and spring onions. These dishes are usually eaten with scoops of flat Arab bread. *Kibbe* are meat balls. Pork is forbidden by Islam, although lamb is popular.

Locally-caught fish is still the staple diet for many Arabs in the Gulf area. The warm shallow waters offer ideal conditions for many fish. As well as commercial fishing-boats, traditional craft of date-palm leaves can still be seen. The fishermen lower their nets round the fish and everyone wades in to drag the nets ashore. Fish is best bought from the markets early in the morning. The choice is enormous: red snapper and kingfish, lobster and huge prawns to name but a few. The fish are sold

Fishermen dragging a net ashore

whole; outside the market, men and boys wait to gut them.

The Bedouin cook meat in a hole in the sand called a *tanour*. A wood fire is lit in the *tanour*. When the fire turns to ashes, the meat is put in—wrapped in leaves—and is covered over with sand. After twenty-four hours, the meat is beautifully tender. It is served on a large dish surrounded by rice and dates. The dish is placed on the ground and everyone sits round it in a circle. The food is always eaten with the right hand. Traditionally, the host offers his guest the choicest pieces.

An Arab meal always ends with coffee, and the traditional preparation of coffee is a symbol of Arab hospitality. The beans are roasted over a fire, before being ground with a pestle and mortar. Water is added to the ground coffee and it is brought to the boil. Sometimes a few cardamom seeds are added, and the coffee is boiled again. It is poured from a *dallah*, a long-spouted coffee pot which is usually made of brass or copper. The coffee is served in small cups without handles. Only a little coffee is poured into each cup. As soon as the guest has finished it, the cup is handed back to the host to be refilled. It is good manners to drink more than one cup. The host will go on refilling the cup until the guest ''jiggles'' it to show that he has had enough. Since alcohol is forbidden by Islam, coffee is a favourite social drink. Coffee is served on all occasions—in the ruler's *majlis* (audience room), in the home, in the office, and often even in shops.

A wedding in the UAE usually lasts about three days. It is

A wedding in Ras al Khaimah. Weddings in the UAE usually last about three days and celebrations are on a large scale

customary to marry a relative. The bride is usually in her late teens. Although her marriage will be arranged by her parents, she may refuse to marry a man who is not acceptable to her.

Wedding celebrations are always on a large scale, with plenty of traditional music and dancing. At celebrations, musicians play drums, *taarah* and *jerba* to accompany the singers. The *taarah* is a tambourine made of goatskin; the *jerba* is a bagpipe

39

Arab musicians playing traditional instruments

made from an inflated goatskin. Sometimes young girls dance between two rows of singers, swinging their long, silky black hair.

At the time of her marriage, a girl is given a dowry by her husband. The dowry is usually a considerable sum of money. The bride keeps this even if she is divorced or widowed. A woman's rights are strictly safeguarded. If she is divorced, she returns to her father's household. (A man may divorce his wife by saying ''I divorce you'' three times.)

Often in the past the bridegroom gave his bride a large wooden chest in which to keep her clothes and jewellery. These chests used to be a typical piece of furniture in Arab homes. They were very heavy, being made of teak or mahogany. Brass-plated and studded varieties are known as Kuwaiti chests.
40

Sometimes the brasswork was highly decorative and elaborate. The chests often had a secret compartment under a false bottom.

Arab jewellery is now usually made of gold, but the traditional jewellery of the Bedouin was made of silver which probably came from Iran. It was heavy and intricately worked, and often had a practical use. The men wore belts of woven silver thread. The decorated *khanjar*, or curved dagger, hung from the belt. The women carried *kohl* (a cosmetic used like today's eyeshadow) in little silver pots. Silver charm-cases, with verses from the Quran sealed inside them, hung on chains around the neck. Heavy anklets and bracelets were worn, and a specific ring for each finger. Tiny objects were often put into hollow silver jewellery to rattle rhythmically with a dancer's movements.

Henna is also associated with weddings and with Eid festivities. It is grown on a bush. The henna berry is dried and ground, and forms a rich red paste when mixed with water. It is used as a form of make-up. On the eve of her wedding, intricate patterns are painted on the hands and feet of the bride. It is also believed that henna possesses medicinal properties and it is sometimes rubbed into the hair to cure headaches.

Folklore has it that Fatima, the daughter of the Prophet Muhammad, was once invited to the wedding of some wealthy people. At the wedding she was mocked for her poverty but the Prophet sent the angels to his daughter with a beautiful dress, a gift of money for the bride, and henna for her own decoration.

The loose-fitting clothes worn by the men and women of the

A bride's hands, painted with intricate patterns in henna

UAE are well adapted to the hot climate. The various layers provide insulation against the heat, and their movement gives a cooling effect. Most of the local men wear a long white gown, called a *dishdasha*, and a headcloth called a *ghutra*. In summer, the *ghutra* is normally a thin white cloth, whilst in winter thicker coloured ones called *shemaghs* are used. A skullcap is usually worn under the *ghutra*. A twisted black coil (*agul*) holds the *ghutra* in place. Sometimes a flowing white or brown cloak known as a *bisht* is worn. It is usually made from camel's wool, and it is edged with gold braid.

Women in the UAE wear loose baggy trousers called *sirwal* under long dresses called *kandura*. The dresses are often

42

embroidered round the neck, sleeves and hem with gold or silver thread. Over the *kandura* is the *thaub*, a rectangular piece of cloth with holes for the arms and head. When women go out, they wear a black cloak (*abaya*) which covers them from head to foot. The Islamic religion requires women to cover their hair in public. Most women also wear veils, and some wear masks called *burqas*.

The women are not only kept apart from men by their clothing. Every house or tent provides a segregated area called a harem. Arab houses are traditionally built around a central courtyard. Often there is a set of two doors to provide a lobby to ensure that guests cannot see directly into the courtyard. The women of the house often go in and out by another door at the back

A woman in Ras al Khaimah wearing the *abaya*—a long black cloak which covers her from head to foot

of the house. A male guest would be shown into the *majlis*—a room for receiving guests. A bathroom would adjoin the *majlis* so that the guest could be entertained without disturbing the privacy of the rest of the house. Traditionally, only a father, a brother, a son, and possibly other very close male relatives, may go beyond the *majlis* to speak with the women of the household.

The family meet in the courtyard, the central area of the house. All the rooms open onto it. There is often a well in the courtyard and cooking is done there. The roof of the house is flat, and it is screened and walled on the outside to provide more space. It is sometimes used for sleeping in summertime. Walls are high, and there are no windows onto the street, or only very small ones high up.

Oil revenue has brought water and electricity to even the most remote areas of the UAE. Nevertheless, the village women still go about their daily routine much as they have always done, although today many of them have Pakistani or Baluchi servants to help them. The women spend their time cooking and tending the animals. A woman never milks a camel; this is traditionally a man's job. In the afternoons the women spin and weave. In the past they made rugs and tents. Nowadays they usually make camel trappings to decorate the camels for the races, for every village has its race track.

Before the introduction of modern low-cost housing, the majority of people on the coast lived in palm-frond houses which were cooled by the sea breeze. In inland towns and villages,

44

A *badgeer,* or windtower—an early form of air-conditioning introduced to the UAE from Persia (the country we now know as Iran)

houses were made of mud bricks. The people from the coast of what is now Iran introduced the *badgeer* or windtower. This was perhaps the earliest form of air conditioning. The Bastakia area of Dubai still contains many of these decorative and distinctive towers. It is called Bastakia because the builders were merchants from Bastak in southern Iran. The tower is divided diagonally to form four triangular shafts. When wind, from any direction, hits one of the walls it is tunnelled down the hollow shaft to the room below, where increased air movement makes the people more comfortable.

Animals of the UAE

There are five different habitats in the UAE—the mountains, the *wadis*, the gravel plains (which run along the foothills of the mountains), the sand desert, and the coastal belt and creeks. Each supports different plants and animals.

The Arabian leopard lives in the isolated Hajar mountains, where it eats wild goats and the Arabian tahr—another goat-like animal. Other local carnivores include the wolf and the caracal. All these animals are extremely rare and shy, and few people have seen them.

There used to be many gazelle. The name *Abu Dhabi* means "father of the white gazelle". Herds of oryx once roamed the sands, but in the 1960s, with the introduction of motor vehicles and good guns, the oryx was wiped out in the UAE. However, there are captive populations, and the public can see them in Al Ain zoo. The oryx has a thick white coat, under which is a fatty layer. The skin is black, which cuts down the absorption of ultra-violet rays from the sun. Wide hooves help the oryx to walk in the sand. The animal has two spiral horns, and it has been suggested that tales of unicorns may really have been descriptions of oryx which had lost a horn!

The little fennec fox is still quite common. It burrows underground where it is cooler, whilst hares find shade beneath a bush or rock. Other small mammals include gerbils, mice and jerboas. They are nocturnal and burrowers, so also escape the heat. Some spiders, such as the fearsome-looking wolf spider and the camel spider, also come out at night. Scorpions are well-suited to the desert conditions. Their hard outer skeletons conserve moisture. In their tails they have a poisonous sting which kills their prey; then they absorb the body juices of their victims. With their jagged claws, they too burrow to keep cool.

More than fifty varieties of reptiles have been recorded in the UAE. They live happily in desert areas because they are cold-blooded, and they are able to take on the temperature of their surroundings. Their scaly skins retain moisture, and they find most of the water they need in the food that they eat. There are many toads in the *wadis*, and in the breeding season thousands of tadpoles can be seen in the streams. Of the snakes, only a few are poisonous, and bites are rare.

The carnivorous monitor lizard lives in the open desert and grows up to 1.2 metres (four feet) long. The thorny-tailed agama lizard inhabits the gravel plains. Although only half the size of the monitor, it looks fierce with sharp teeth and strong jaws, a long spiky tail which it lashes vigorously, and an ability to

47

The thorny-tailed agama lizard which inhabits the gravel plains

inflate its body and hiss loudly. However, it is in fact a vegetarian! The most common reptile is probably the gecko. Most houses play host to a few of these sandy-coloured lizards, and they are usually welcomed since they eat the insects.

Some freshwater fish live in the mountain *wadis*, and the sea is rich in marine life. The dugong (a seal-like sea-cow) is seen, but only rarely. It was this creature which inspired tales of mermaids, because of the way it floats in the water.

With such a long coastline, the UAE has always been important in the migration of seabirds. A number of birds also live in the oases and date plantations. Today, well over three hundred species of birds have been recorded in the UAE. The programme of "turning the desert green" has encouraged many more birds to "stop over" and some of them also breed in the UAE. Planting has produced vegetable matter which attracts insects, and they in turn attract the birds. The UAE is in an excellent position for birds migrating from Europe to Africa and from Asia to Africa to stop and take a rest. Many have found the Emirates a good place in which to winter. Few birds spend the entire year here, but some of those which are frequently seen are palm doves, house sparrows, parakeets, mynahs and hoopoes. The Egyptian vulture lives and breeds in the mountains near Al Ain. There are also four varieties of big, impressive-looking eagles.

Since bees are native to the desert, the bee-eater can also be found here. It is an interesting bird. It wipes the bee on the branch of a tree in order to knock off the insect's sting. Since it is not immune to bee-stings, it plays safe and treats all insects in this way. The "butcher" bird is also seen here. It impales its food on the spikes of thorn trees.

Along the coast, millions of Socotra cormorants and black-headed gulls can be seen. Waders, such as herons and flamingos, are also found in abundance. Dubai's creek attracts the flamingos, and a man-made island is being planned for them.

His Highness Sheikh Mohammed bin Rashid al Maktoum established the Dubai Wildlife Research Centre in 1982. The Centre specializes in projects aimed at conserving the wildlife of the Arabian region. Already a remarkable record of rearing hubara bustards from wild-laid eggs has been achieved. In this way, stocks of hubara depleted by hunting can be replenished.

49

The bird most often associated with Arab countries is, perhaps, the falcon. For centuries, falconry has been the most popular way of hunting small game.Falconry probably originated in the steppes and dunes of Central Asia. It grew in importance in the Islamic world following the Muslim conquests, which brought the Arabs into contact with Byzantines and Persians.

The peregrine falcon, renowned for its courage and high flight, is a favourite. It is caught in the Emirates on its autumnal migration from Pakistan to Africa. Sakers and lanners are also used.

The chief quarry in the Emirates is the hubara or MacQueen's bustard. The hubara is several times larger than the hawk, and the sport is rarely one-sided. It can squirt a slime onto the hawk's feathers and eyes. The hawk is temporarily blinded, and the sticky substance glues its feathers together so that it cannot fly properly. Sometimes the hubara will sit perfectly still, hoping that the hawk will not spot him, but a well-trained hawk knows its quarry is lying low, and bides its time. Even when cornered, the hubara will put up a hard fight. Sometimes it manages to outfly the hawk, and the falconer must call back his bird by swinging the lure. A good hawk can take up to nine hubara in a day.

There are two traditional methods of catching falcons. One is to erect a thin net and loosely peg it to the ground in an area where the birds are known to hunt. A pigeon is tied under the net to attract the falcon. When the falcon dives down on its prey,

Falconry — still the most popular way of hunting small game in the UAE

the net is pulled from the ground and the bird becomes entangled in it.

In the second method a captive pigeon is again used to attract the falcon. This time the Bedouin digs a pit and hides in it, holding a string attached to the decoy pigeon. When the falcon is sighted, the pigeon is encouraged to flutter. The falcon swoops on the pigeon and kills it. Sometimes a net is employed. The Bedouin jerks another string and the net snaps over the bird. Otherwise, the Bedouin simply eases the dead pigeon, with the falcon feeding on it, towards the pit. When the falcon is sufficiently close, it is caught by the legs. A great deal of time and patience is required to trap a bird. Female birds are

51

preferred because they are larger, as is the case with all birds of prey.

A bird can be trained in two to three weeks. Her eyelids are sealed with thread and she is hooded with a leather cap or *burqa*. This cuts off the sight of any alarming movements. The eyelids are gradually unsealed as she becomes familiar with her owner. Stepping onto the fist is encouraged by tempting her with meat. As the bird becomes tamer, her owner calls her along a line tied to the "jesses" on her legs. The jesses are straps, usually made of leather. However, the Bedouin of the Emirates braid the straps from camel or goat's hair since the humidity in the climate encourages mould growth on leather. The falcon is

"Manning" a falcon. This is part of a falcon's training, enabling it to get used to people and noise

trained to come to a lure made of hubara wings which it quickly learns to associate with the meals it gets when it lands on the lure.

Under Islamic law a Muslim cannot eat "dead" meat—that is, meat that has not been killed specifically for the purpose of eating. However, the Quran allows the falcon's kill to be eaten if the hunter releases his bird "in the name of Allah". The falcon is allowed a bite at her kill, but then the kill is cunningly removed. If the falcon were allowed to satisfy her appetite, she would not hunt again that day.

Falcons can reach twenty years old. Some hunt right up until they are eighteen. At the end of winter, eighty per cent of birds are traditionally released back into the wild. Only the star performers are kept. Although some birds fetch very high prices, to an Arab their worth is immeasurable.

Dubai now boasts a falcon hospital—the first of its kind in the world—built by Finance and Industry Minister, H. H. Sheikh Hamdan bin Rashid al Maktoum. It is run by an American veterinary surgeon, who has been a keen falconer himself for the last twenty-five years. The hospital is equipped with a special X-ray unit. In the laboratory, blood samples are examined. Culture and sensitivity tests are carried out to make sure that the bacteria are sensitive to a medicine, so that the right anti-biotic is prescribed for each sick bird. Some innovative surgery is also performed at the hospital. A common ailment is infected feet (known to the Bedouin as *somal* or "bumble foot"), when the feet have been accidentally pierced by the bird's

53

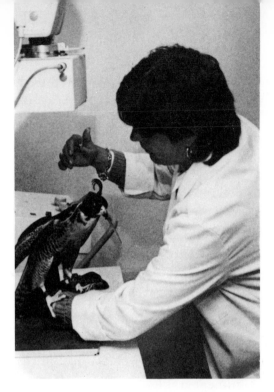

talons. After surgery, the bird is fitted with a hollowed-out plaster cast and looks as if she is wearing a high-heeled shoe. This clever device ensures that there is no pressure on the foot. Falcons sometimes suffer from fungus of the lungs. This is treated in an oxygen cage, as we would treat a patient with pneumonia in an oxygen tent.

At the height of the hunting season, in December, there may be as many as thirty-five birds in the hospital. People bring their birds to the hospital from all over the Gulf.

The birds are fed once a day on quails, since quails quickly convert food into body weight. Once a week, sometimes more, the falcons are encouraged to kill the quails for themselves.

Otherwise, being very sensitive birds, falcons can become unhappy and self-destructive. Just as nervous people will bite their nails so a falcon will bite its claws. They are flown every day, and their quarters are "carpeted" with sand to make them feel at home. The peregrines at the hospital live in modified daylight, and they are given extra hormones to encourage them to moult since the climate in the UAE is poor for moulting.

DOMESTICATED ANIMALS

Deserts are the most difficult places in the world for animals to survive in. The days are long and hot, there is little water and often food is scarce. So creatures which live here have developed ways of coping with these problems. One animal which is ideally suited to its surroundings is the camel. No one knows when camels were first domesticated but today there are none in the wild, nor have there been for hundreds of years. Every camel in the UAE is accounted for and has its owner's mark upon it to prove it.

The camel used by the Bedouin of the UAE is the dromedary or one-humped camel. It well deserves its nickname of "ship of the desert". Its large flat feet can move easily over the sand without sinking. It will always sit facing the sun so that the smallest amount of body area is exposed to the sun's rays. During the heat of the day, it conserves its energy by sitting quite still, with much of its body resting in the cooler ground below the top soil. Its hump stores fat, which can be used to supply energy if needed. The camel's hump is a sign of its

55

physical condition. When the camel is well-fed, its hump is plump and firm. The hump sags as the fat is used up when food is scarce. A camel can drink as much as 120 litres (27 gallons) of water at a time. In other animals, the blood cells would burst and the animal would die. But a camel loses water from its tissues and not from its blood so there is no strain on its heart. If it lacks water, it can adjust its body temperature to that of its surroundings, and thereby avoid sweating. It can go for several days without food and water, and even in the height of summer has been known to survive for as long as seventeen days without water.

In the desert, water is usually found some distance below the surface and has to be drawn up in goatskin bags. Imagine how many bags of water each camel drinks. Watering a herd of perhaps fifty camels in summertime would be very hard work indeed. But in the winter camels may go for six, or even seven, weeks without any water if there is enough of the right kind of grazing.

The camel has double rows of long, heavy lashes to protect its eyes from wind-blown sand. It can also close its nostrils to keep out the sand. It has a keen sense of sight and smell. Its coat insulates it against the sun during the day and keeps it warm in the cool of the night.

In the past, the Bedouin's livelihood depended on his camels. For much of the year he lived mainly on camel's milk and dried dates. Camel's milk is high in vitamin C, and a healthy female can give five litres (nine pints) a day as well as suckling her calf.

The camel was also used for riding and as a beast of burden. The Bedouin travelled light, with rifle and *khanjar* (curved dagger), a few cooking-pots, some dried dates, and as many goatskin bags of water as the camels could carry. The Bedouin always thought of his camel's wellbeing first. The animals would be watered at the wells first. Even when he was in a hurry he would allow his camels to wander for grazing. Nowadays, camels are fed on locally-grown alfalfa, but the boys who look after them still gather the natural desert grasses for them as well. The heat makes salt a necessary ingredient in their diet, and many bushes in the desert are naturally salty.

The camel is, of course, a source of meat; its wool is used for making rugs, and its hide for making containers. No part of it is wasted—even the dung is used for fuel. Since the female gives milk and is also considered the faster runner, a herd consists mainly of females. The Bedouin would generally kill male calves for a festive occasion, such as a wedding. Camels would also be traded for rifles, rice, coffee and jewellery. A Bedouin's camels were a sign of his wealth.

Traditionally, the camel was hobbled by having its front legs tied together to prevent it from wandering too far. The Arabic word for "string" sounds like "hobble", so perhaps this is where the English word comes from. Unfortunately, with more and more cars on the road, the camels sometimes meet their death at the hands of motorists. The wide highway connecting Abu Dhabi Emirate to Dubai Emirate is notorious for this. The long, straight road encourages fast driving but the desert on either side of the road is unlit at nights. A camel will suddenly loom up out of the pitch blackness and shamble into the road. By the time the driver sees it, it is too late.

Another domesticated animal used in the UAE is the donkey. Like the camel, it is a beast of burden, and can be seen even now pulling water-carts in remote areas.

Horses are not commonly used in the UAE, as the ground is too soft for their hooves. However, in the past, merchant families in the towns sometimes owned and rode horses. Arab horses are famous throughout the world for their spirit and

A Bedouin watering his camels. In the past, a Bedouin's livelihood depended almost entirely on his camels

Camels—their long, heavy lashes protect their eyes from sand

stamina, and for their good looks. They were already known at the time of the Prophet Muhammad. With the spread of Islam, they found their way to North Africa, Spain and France and, after the Crusades, to Northern Europe, notably Britain. Most sheikhs like to own some, and horses have always been considered a suitable gift between sheikhs.

Sometimes, a few cattle are kept in the oases, and in Buraimi oasis oxen are also kept to plough the fields because wheat grows there.

Sheep and goats are still herded in the UAE. Goats are preferred as they eat almost anything. The government pays families an allowance for every animal they raise. The women milk the goats, and some of the milk is turned into curds. The goat hair used to be woven into tent material, and into socks

59

A goat for sale at a market. The government pays an allowance for every animal raised and goats are still herded in large numbers

to protect the feet from burning sands. The skins became water-carriers. A musical instrument, rather like the Scottish bagpipes, was also fashioned from it. Even the hooves were used. Fastened onto a piece of cloth and worn by the men round their waist and over the hips during traditional dances, they sounded like castanets as they clacked together.

From Pearls to Black Gold—
Trade and Industry in the UAE

Pearl diving used to be the main occupation of people living along the shores of the Arabian Gulf. At the turn of the nineteenth century, at the pearling trade's peak, a flotilla of some twelve hundred boats was home to about twenty-two thousand sailors. This meant that most of the Trucial States' able-bodied male population was engaged in pearling.

Dhow is the general term used to cover all local craft. The pearling boats were called *sambuks*. They were propelled by sails, but they had oars as well. The *sambuk* was made ready by oiling the upper hull with shark oil, and anti-fouling the lower half of the hull with a mixture of lime and sheep's fat. Supplies of dates, rice, tea, sugar, coffee and water for the crew were stored on board.

The ship's captain was called the *nakhuda*. He collected together a crew of between forty and sixty men and set out for the diving place, known as the *heer*. The life of the diver was hard and dangerous. Hazards of the sea included giant stingrays,

61

swordfish and jellyfish. To prevent himself from being stung the diver sometimes wore a white cotton suit. Leather finger stalls, called *khabt*, protected his fingers. A leather socket covered the big toe of his right foot which the diver used to push his way along the seabed. He pinched his nose with a peg of horn or bone to keep out the water. His only other equipment was a knife to prise the oysters from the seabed, and a basket, hung round his neck, to carry them in. When he jumped he had two ropes tied round his waist, one weighted to sink him, the other by which his assistant—the *saib*—could pull him up.

Work began shortly after sunrise. First, the oysters caught the previous day would be opened. Perhaps one pearl would be found in four thousand oysters. A dive might last a minute and a half, though an experienced diver could stay under water for up to four minutes. The more perfect pearls generally came from the deeper water. After a few minutes' rest the diver would go down again. This routine could continue for six to eight hours. Diving was not permitted during Ramadan.

Pearls were sold to the *tawwash*, the buying merchant, accompanied by traditional bargaining. The captain negotiated the sale, but he was accompanied by two of his crew to see fair play. Negotiations were carried out through finger language under a piece of cloth in order to keep the deal private. The merchant used delicate scales and weights of the semi-precious stones agate and cornelian. The pearls were sieved for size through small perforated copper basins.

During the last century, Gulf merchants sent their pearls to

A fish market. Fish is still the staple diet of many Arabs in the UAE

Bombay which was the great eastern centre of the trade. Buyers from Europe and New York called there regularly.

By 1940 the pearl trade had almost disappeared due to Japan's development of the cultured pearl and the lack of demand for such luxuries as pearls during the Depression of the 1930s. However, fishing has continued to be an important source of livelihood, especially in the Northern Emirates.

The variety of fish found in and around the coast is enormous. Fishermen can be at sea for as long as a week before returning to the fish markets with their catches. The annual catch is about 70,000 tonnes, some of which is dried and exported.

Fish has always been a favourite food of the Gulf Arabs. In the past, it was the main source of protein for many people. However, some popular varieties of fish have decreased in supply. For this reason, the UAE government, with Japanese assistance, has set up the country's first fish-farming project. The National Mariculture Centre is in Umm al Qawain. There are forty ponds of different sizes for breeding popular varieties. The Centre also comprises a laboratory and an aquarium, where about fifty species of Gulf fish are on display.

The transformation of the UAE's economy began in 1962 with the first export of oil from Abu Dhabi.

This "black gold" was formed under the surface of the earth millions of years ago. It has long been known to man, yet it is only during the past hundred years or so that we have realized its usefulness.

Today, oil is used for transportation and heating, and in the manufacture of fertilizers, fabrics, medicines, plastics, pesticides, paints and thousands of other items. No wonder, then, that having such a precious commodity makes a country powerful.

The Middle East is one of the main oil-producing regions in the world, extracting about one-third of the world's oil. The UAE, however, was a latecomer to the ranks of the world's major oil-exporting countries with Abu Dhabi exporting its first barrel of oil only in 1962. The Abu Dhabi National Oil Company (ADNOC) was founded nine years later, in 1971. It has a monopoly over distribution and is responsible for all petroleum installations and oil-based industries in the Emirate.

Dubai is the second largest producer in the UAE. In 1963, Conoco formed the Dubai Petroleum Company (DPC) which concentrates on offshore production. Fateh is the largest and the oldest of the four DPC oilfields. Sheikh Rashid personally named the field when it was discovered in 1966. *Fateh* means "good fortune" in Arabic. In May 1982, a major new onshore discovery was made in the Margham field.

The Mubarak offshore oilfield in Sharjah was discovered in 1972 but the first shipment was not exported until almost two years later. The field's production capacity gradually fell. However, in December 1980, a much-needed boost came with Amoco's discovery of a major oil and gas field just a short distance from Sharjah itself.

In the Emirate of Ras al Khaimah, oil was struck in the Saleh field, some forty-two kilometres (twenty-six miles) offshore, in February 1983. The other Emirates continue to grant concessions for oil and gas exploration.

In 1983, Abu Dhabi produced about 850,000 barrels a day—that is 69 per cent of the UAE's output. Dubai produced between 330,000 and 360,000 barrels a day (29.5 per cent of the UAE's output) and Sharjah over 50,000 barrels a day (0.5 per cent). A large proportion of crude oil is exported, mainly to Japan. The USA, France and the Netherlands are also major customers, and Britain and West Germany take a small amount.

The distribution of refined products is the responsibility of the Emirates General Petroleum Corporation (EGPC). The

An offshore oil-rig. The discovery of this "black gold" has transformed the economy of the UAE

EGPC came into being in January 1981 and took over petroleum stations previously operated by BP, Shell and Caltex. It operates from Dubai. In Abu Dhabi, petroleum products are distributed by an ADNOC subsidiary which has a small refinery at Umm al Nar island, and a larger facility at Ruwais.

At present, Abu Dhabi and Dubai are the main producers of liquefied natural gas in the Gulf. Abu Dhabi's plant on Das Island is operated by Abu Dhabi Gas Liquefaction Company (ADGAS). The gas is separated into liquid gas—propane and butane—and dry gas. Liquid gas is exported mainly to Japan, where it is used in the manufacture of chemicals and fuels. The residue dry gas is used to supply local industry.

During the 1970s, Dubai's natural gas was flared off, but in 1980 a gas treatment plant, owned by the Dubai Natural Gas Company (DUGAS), began operations. This now supplies some ninety per cent of the fuel needs of the Dubai Aluminium Company (DUBAL), and around five per cent of the fuel for the Dubai Electricity Company's power station at Jebel Ali.

DUBAL is one of the world's most energy-efficient industrial operations. In 1983 it produced 151,170 tonnes of aluminium, its main sales being to Japan, Iran, Korea and the USA. DUBAL helps the Emirate to conserve its resources of both energy and water by utilizing waste heat from its power station gas turbines.

Associated with the aluminium smelter is a desalination plant. Desalination is the process by which fresh water is obtained from seawater. This is done by heating the seawater so that some of it evaporates, forming water vapour. The vapour rises and is piped into colder condenser tubes. It drops as distilled water into trays, and is then led away for blending to produce drinking water. For every unit of fresh water produced DUBAL pumps in eight units of seawater. DUBAL supplies some 67 per cent of Dubai's water requirements. Desalination is very important in the desert, where water supply from rainfall is insufficient.

At Jebel Ali there are also cement works, a structural steelwork fabrication workshop, a 300-megawatt steam power station, and an electrical cable plant. It is envisaged that this extensive

An aerial view of the Abu Dhabi gas liquefaction plant

industrial development, thirty-five kilometres (twenty-two miles) south-west of Dubai, will serve as the oilfield supply and distribution centre for the Middle East. The central facility is the largest man-made port in the world.

Mina Jebel Ali can take sixty-seven ships and has fifteen kilometres (nine miles) of quays. It was completed towards the end of 1980. The port has been designated a Free Trade Zone to encourage trading and re-exporting in the Middle East. Some of the benefits include exemption from taxes, duty-free import of machinery and materials needed for industry, and no currency restrictions. Cargo can be placed in storage, duty-free, until favourable market conditions arise. In the Free Trade Zone there is a modern container terminal, extensive transit storage areas and warehouses. There is also a temperature-controlled

68

warehouse for delicate cargoes which would deteriorate in ordinary storage conditions.

Before the oil boom, the coastline of the UAE had few harbours and ports. The shallow waters and sandy flats meant that large ocean-going tankers had to lie offshore and transfer their cargo into lighter vessels. Prior to harbour developments in Abu Dhabi, Dubai was the only port of entry for merchandise. For centuries, there was a thriving pearling and trading port in Dubai, sheltered in the natural creek. The ancient *dhows* still ply the creek today. The UAE depends heavily on imports for its development needs. Imports through Dubai increased sevenfold between 1964 and 1972. Today, two-thirds of the UAE's imports pass through Dubai. Japan is the leading supplier. The United States, the United Kingdom, West Germany and Italy are also major suppliers.

One of the first things Sheikh Rashid of Dubai decided to do with oil revenue was to build a fifteen-berth port. Even before its completion, however, it became clear that it would need to be larger to meet the needs of Dubai's expanding trade. The number of berths was increased to thirty-seven. Completed in October 1972, it was appropriately named Port Rashid.

Sharjah and Ras al Khaimah also have ports, whilst Khor Fakkan, an enclave of Sharjah Emirate on the east coast, has a deep-water container terminal. At Jebel Dhanna, in Abu Dhabi Emirate, there is the vital oil export terminal.

Dubai's strategic location near the entrance of the Arabian Gulf makes it the ideal site for a ship repair yard for the many

An aerial view of Port Rashid

ships using the oil route. In December 1973, work began on the dry dock. One of the largest in the world, it stands at the mouth of Dubai Creek. Today, tugs help to bring ships into the port, where they can be cleaned and repaired. The dry dock is equipped to repair even the largest tanker afloat. It is particularly suitable for heavy offshore equipment, such as the jack-up platforms, derricks and pipe-laying barges so vital to the oilfields. At the other end of the creek lies Al Jadaf Ship Docking Yard which opened in July 1978. Here traditional Arab *dhows* are repaired alongside huge cargo liners.

A symbol of the UAE's trading history is the International Trade Centre in Dubai. This thirty-nine storey, 200-metre (650-foot) high tower is a striking landmark which dominates the skyline. It opened in 1979 and houses over one hundred national and international companies. The complex also includes the Hilton International Hotel, three apartment blocks and two exhibition halls. Businessmen come here from Saudi Arabia, Kuwait, Bahrain, Qatar, Oman and even further afield.

A vital feature of trade is banking. The unit of currency in the UAE is the *dirham*. This was created in 1973 to replace the Bahraini *dinar* and the Qatar/Dubai *riyal* which had been used previously in the Emirates.

Foreign banks flocked to the UAE in the 1970s and banking grew out of proportion to the population. In 1973 a central

Dubai dry dock

monetary authority, the UAE Currency Board, was established. This was replaced in 1980 by the Central Bank. The rulers of Abu Dhabi and Dubai agreed to place half of their national revenues with the new institution. This example of unity gives the Central Bank the federal support which the Currency Board lacked. The Central Bank has the power to regulate operations of the financial system. Banking can no longer grow in the previous uncontrolled way. Restrictions have been enforced so that all foreign banks have had to reduce the number of their branches to a maximum of eight. Now banking is dominated by national banks. In 1983, the Emirates Industrial Bank was

The International Trade Centre in Dubai

A cement works in Ras al Khaimah with the barren and rugged Hajar mountains in the background

established to provide loans to new and expanding industries.

Though the economy of the UAE depends heavily on oil and oil-based industries, the government is well aware of the dangers of relying on one single source of income. One of the aims of the Chambers of Commerce is to encourage new industries. Industrial development has come in a natural manner in tune with emerging needs. Consequently, a number of plants were established to manufacture building materials in order to meet the needs of the construction boom. Cement factories sprang up through the Emirates. The largest is in Ras al Khaimah. Using the rocks of the Hajar mountains, Ras al Khaimah has also established an export business in aggregates (the broken stones and other materials used in making concrete). Light

73

industries in the UAE include the manufacture of ballpoint pens, paper bags, rope, paint and foam. Aluminium products such as sheds, doors and water-tanks are made, as are iron and steel products.

Similarly, many plants were established for manufacturing foodstuffs in order to supply the market with local products in place of imported ones. These include ice-cream, cooking oil, nuts and crisps, and canned drinks. The Emirates Macaroni Factory turns out seven thousand tonnes of pasta a year. Dairies produce milk, yoghurt, *labneh* (a thick, creamy curd) and cheese. There are plants which bottle mineral waters from the freshwater springs at Ras al Khaimah, Masafi and Hatta. At the same time, great attention has been paid to agriculture.

Turning the Desert Green

Traditionally, agriculture in the UAE centred on the nomads, who travelled the deserts in search of pasture for their animals, and on small oases, where crops such as dates could be grown.

Dates are still a major crop. The date palm has separate male and female plants and is propagated from root suckers produced by the female plants. The fruit is high in calorific value and used to be the staple food for men and beasts on long journeys through the desert. The tree trunks were used in the construction of houses, and branches were bound together to make a lightweight building material known as *barasti*. The leaves were woven to make baskets.

Date gardens were planted where watering by *aflaj* was possible. *Aflaj* are ancient underground water channels which were probably constructed in pre-Islamic times. The *falaj* (the singular of *aflaj*) brings water from its source to the date gardens where it comes to the surface. The flow can then be directed and regulated.

In *falaj*-irrigated gardens, a few other fruit trees grew among the date palms. Oranges, lemons and limes were the most common. Mangoes, figs, mulberries, bananas and pomegranates also seemed to do well and grapes were sometimes grown over trellises. Beneath the trees, several crops of alfalfa (a crop grown to feed cattle and camels) could be harvested each year, and some vegetables also grew.

Date gardens in desert locations grew without *falaj* irrigation, for the roots of the date palms quickly reached down to the water table. However, the resulting fruits were smaller. *Barasti* fencing protected the gardens from drifting sand.

In Ras al Khaimah and Fujeirah, better rainfall and a higher underground water table made a larger amount of land

76

cultivable. Here, the traditions of fishing and date-farming were largely untouched by the oil boom.

Despite the extreme aridity of most of the UAE, the country is now producing a large proportion of its own food. Experiments both in cattle-raising and in growing a variety of crops prove steadily more successful. Farmers and agriculturalists have come up with ingenious irrigation systems, greenhouses that keep the heat out rather than in, and hydroponic farms. This last is a system whereby plants are grown without soil in plastic tubes. They are kept in temperature-controlled greenhouses and fed by liquids pumped through the tubes. Tomatoes and cucumbers grown in this way can be harvested after a few weeks.

Digdagga Agricultural Trial Station was set up in 1955 in Ras al Khaimah to find out which crops would grow best in the harsh climate. Various vegetables and then fruit trees were tried out. An agricultural school was opened. Digdagga is still a thriving area.

The Arid Lands Research Centre was set up in 1972 on Sadiyat Island in Abu Dhabi. Experiments in hydroponics are undertaken here.

Another flourishing agricultural centre is Al Ain oasis, the birthplace of President Sheikh Zayed. Here there are about one thousand farms. Many of them were developed at the government's expense and then allocated to the people. Agricultural guidance centres and veterinary centres encourage the country's farmers, and the government helps with the cost of fertilizers, seeds and pesticides.

Date palms in Fujeirah

In 1975 the government asked the United Nations Food and Agricultural Organization (FAO) to help. Their findings assisted the UAE in planning for the future. FAO experts train local people to continue the work.

Experiments to discover the most suitable methods of irrigation are particularly important in the desert where water is scarce. It has been found that drip irrigation works best for rows of vegetable crops; the bubbler system for fruit trees; and sprinklers for alfalfa, onions and potatoes. Rhodes grass, from Kenya, is also grown and made into hay. Imagine climbing to the top of a desert sand dune and finding a field of wheat stretched out below you. That is what you would find at Al Oha near Al Ain. Such a surprise is no longer as uncommon as it might sound in the UAE. By the year 2000, the country hopes

78

to be able to grow all the wheat it needs to feed its people.

The number of farmers in the UAE increased from over 7,500 in 1977 to 12,500 in 1983. Production of field crops increased by 500 per cent between 1977 and 1982. In the same period, fruit production rose by 284 per cent, while vegetable production rose by 300 per cent. Vegetables grown in the UAE include cabbages, beans, lettuce, eggplant (aubergines), tomatoes, peppers, cucumbers and potatoes. Tobacco is also grown. Ras al Khaimah and Fujeirah produce a variety of fruits ranging from lemons to bananas and mangoes. Watermelon and sweet melon also thrive.

There are a number of poultry and dairy farms in the UAE.

Market stalls full of locally-grown produce—the result of a dramatic increase in agricultural production

Supermarkets now stock locally produced eggs and chickens, and the country is well on its way to self-sufficiency in this area. Fresh milk and yoghurt come from Al Ain, Umm al Qawain and Al Marmum in the Emirate of Dubai, as well as from Digdagga. Dairies use an instant cooling system to make fresh milk last longer.

The rapid expansion of agriculture meant that many new wells were dug for irrigation. This resulted in the level of the water table dropping dramatically in many areas. To cope with this, the production of desalinated water has been increased. The government now controls the drilling of wells. Another major step is the construction of dams to catch the water from the mountains which would otherwise rush down the *wadis* to the sea. Progress is also being achieved in the recycling of sewage

A roundabout in Abu Dhabi. Sheikh Zayed's dream of "turning the desert green" has led to colourful parks and gardens being planted throughout the Emirates

to provide water to irrigate parks and gardens. The President, Sheikh Zayed, dreams of turning the desert green, and this no longer seems as unlikely as it sounds. So far, Abu Dhabi, the nation's capital, is the greenest city, but this greenness is fast spreading throughout the UAE.

"Sweet soil" (that is fertile desert soil untainted by salt from the sea) is brought to sites; then organic matter—such as treated sludge or cow dung—is added to it to nourish it. The municipalities run nurseries to provide shrubs, plants and trees for public parks and gardens. City residents can obtain plants free or at minimal cost for their own gardens. Roadsides and roundabouts in the Emirates are now ablaze with colour, as periwinkles, sun-plants and marigolds bloom. Bougainvillea is probably the most colourful garden plant, whilst oleander, jasmine and hibiscus also thrive. Leafy Indian almond trees and tall eucalyptus flourish and give shade. All this in a land which not so long ago was little more than sand.

The Facilities and Achievements of the UAE

There is no use for money if it is not dedicated to the service of the people.

PRESIDENT SHEIKH ZAYED

With the discovery of oil, and the ensuing wealth, the UAE has developed at an amazing pace. The federal government has constructed a welfare system to match any in the world.

The country's first school opened in Sharjah in 1953. In 1971, education was made compulsory, for boys and girls alike, from the age of six. Education is free for all nationals, even for those studying abroad. Meals, uniforms and textbooks are also free. Each child receives pocket money which increases with his progress at school each year. In addition, parents receive a monthly allowance for each child who is attending full-time school.

The government's policy is to take the benefits of modern civilization out to the Bedouin, rather than force the Bedouin to come to the cities. There are now a number of small schools

82

A girls' school in Abu Dhabi. Education is free for all children in the UAE

in remote rural areas. And, in this way, the Bedouin's traditional way of life is not disrupted.

Besides government-owned schools there are a number of private schools in the UAE. English-speaking education is also available, and there are schools of other nationalities including French, German and Japanese. In accordance with Islam, co-education amongst Muslims is only at the very youngest ages, and instruction in the Islamic religion is compulsory. Evening classes for adults are also encouraged.

In 1977, the country's first university opened in Al Ain. It started with four faculties: Humanities and Social Sciences,

Natural Sciences, Education and Public Administration, and Political Science. The faculty of Islamic Law was added in 1978, and those of Agriculture and Engineering during 1980-1981. It is a segregated university, the women's college being some distance from the main section. The majority of students are from the UAE itself; others come from other parts of the Gulf.

Many students also go abroad every year to study in other Arab countries, or in Europe or America. In addition, there are training facilities in many of the large companies, especially in the oil sector. ADNOC, for instance, runs a Career Development Centre. In this way the UAE is able to rely more and more on its own trained people to fill important posts.

The government is also making efforts to train women as educators and teachers, and thus reduce dependence on foreign teaching staff. The Ministry of Labour and Social Affairs supports and promotes the progress of local women. Her Highness Sheikha Fatima, the President's wife, heads the UAE Women's Federation. Eleven Social Development Centres in the Emirates provide teaching in health, nutrition, child care, language-training in Arabic and English, cultural and religious lectures and demonstrations. Local traditional handicrafts are encouraged. They include weaving, *talli* work (a type of braiding used to decorate local costume), and plaiting date-palm fibres which are sewn together to form mats, bowls and baskets.

Other women are employed by the police force. They handle criminal investigations concerning women and juveniles. They also conduct airport searches of women and driving tests for

84

Weaving and *talli* work — examples of traditional handicrafts which are being encouraged by the government of the UAE

women. Some women are also involved in broadcasting in the UAE.

Every community of more than one thousand people in the UAE has its own clinic; and special travelling clinics visit the nomadic Bedouin in the desert. Each Emirate has at least one hospital. Some of the most modern and best-equipped hospitals in the world are to be found in Abu Dhabi, Dubai and Al Ain.

At the time of independence, the UAE was prone to a number of fatal diseases. Now, with a thorough preventive medicine

85

Policewomen on parade in Dubai

programme, cholera, typhoid and tuberculosis are gradually being eliminated. The UAE was one of the first countries in the Middle East to be declared free of smallpox. The country can also boast its own medical pioneer. Dr. Moinul Haq, the opthalmic consultant at Dubai's Rashid Hospital, invented the technique of grafting fish corneas into human eyes.

Major highways through the desert link the Emirates and each city has a modern road system. The UAE is well provided with port facilities which are vital to a country's prosperity. There are also four major international airports—at Abu Dhabi,

Dubai, Sharjah and Ras al Khaimah—as well as a number of military airfields. In 1985, a national airline called "Emirates" was launched. It is based in Dubai.

Although there is a public bus service in the UAE, taxis are the main form of public transport. There is no rail system. The majority of families possess at least one car of their own and very often they have a 4-wheel drive vehicle in order to cope with rough terrain in the desert and the rural areas.

There are telephone, cable and telex facilities throughout the UAE, and the car telephone service is becoming popular. Public payphones appeared early in 1982. It is possible to dial direct to many different countries all over the world.

There are four radio stations and two television stations in the UAE, and Abu Dhabi and Dubai operate English-language services. The UAE Coastal Radio Service opened in September

Dubai airport—one of the four major international airports

1982. There is a flourishing Arabic press in the country as well as three English-language daily newspapers.

Only a few years ago, power cuts were not uncommon in the Emirates, especially during the hot summer months when air conditioning is in maximum use. Now, power cuts are a thing of the past since power stations have grown to meet the demands. Electricity is subsidized and the government makes sure everyone is provided with good housing, running water and electricity.

The policy of the country is to share the benefits of its wealth so that the quality of life is improved for everyone—not merely for the nation's own people but for developing countries which require foreign aid. This is a belief based on the precepts of Islam. As a result, the UAE gives generously to countries throughout Africa and Asia.

Sports and Leisure

Sports and leisure facilities have been developed to such an extent that the UAE manages to surprise most of its visitors. It is not surprising for the sun and sea to go hand in hand with water sports such as swimming, sailing, windsurfing, water-skiing, fishing and scuba diving. But Grand Prix motor-racing, cycling, hockey and cricket are much more unexpected.

Football is definitely the number one sport. Spontaneous games are played on any vacant patch of sand, as well as the organized ones in the splendid stadiums. There is a UAE Football Association and the UAE National League is the main feature of the season.

Perhaps the most surprising sport of all to be found in the desert is ice-hockey! The first ice rink opened in 1979, and there are regular ice shows, featuring both local and international stars.

Other sports include tennis, polo, squash, netball, basketball, karting, archery, and tenpin bowling. Most of the large hotels house gymnasiums, and there are many well-equipped clubs. An annual raft race takes place every November. The craft are appropriately constructed from empty oil drums! A more traditional race is the long-boat race, with each boat manned by upwards of eighty rowers.

One of the more traditional sports to be found in the UAE is camel racing. A young camel can be trained for racing when it is three to four years old. It is led slowly round the track alongside a more mature camel to set a good example. Camels can be stubborn, and training can take a few months. The rider is always a small, light boy.

At the start of a race, the trainers, mounted on other camels, calm the new racers. There is an unwritten law that a camel may only be whipped into action at the start and the end of a race. A camel averages twenty-five kilometres (over fifteen miles) an hour. Nowadays, a trainer sometimes instructs the jockey by closed circuit radio as he watches the race on television from the stand.

Buying a racing camel is carried out with as much care as buying a racehorse. Its feet and legs, its height and girth, are carefully examined. Its lineage, too, is studied. Thoroughbreds have been known to fetch vast sums of money. The most famous pedigree is the Aseel, which means "pure".

Today, camel racing has become a very competitive business, with established racetracks and stadiums. Although betting or gambling is forbidden under Islam, camels may race for prizes. The prizes usually consist of a 4-wheel drive vehicle and a sum

A camel race. Camel racing is a major sport in the UAE

of money. Even the smallest village has a camel racing track close by. For sheikh and Bedouin alike, camels and camel racing are a part of the Arab way of life.

With so much to offer in the way of sporting and leisure facilities, it is not surprising that tourism has begun to play a part in the economy of the UAE. The climate, naturally, has helped to develop this new industry. The sun-seekers of Europe can escape from their own cold winters to guaranteed sunshine. This, combined with excellent hotels, beautiful beaches, spectacular scenery and the country's interesting history and culture, makes for an excellent holiday.

However, the attractions of the UAE are not, as yet, widely known. Sometimes the media reports have an adverse effect on a country. For instance, front-page news of an oil slick in the area is off-putting, even though the beaches of the UAE may not have suffered from it. Again, the Iran-Iraq war has been sufficient deterrent to some would-be tourists because of the nearness of Iran to the UAE—although the actual border of Iran with Iraq is some considerable distance from the UAE. However, shipping problems further up the Gulf arising from the war have not made any noticeable impact in the UAE. In fact, problems in Iran's southern ports have given the UAE's facilities a chance to attract new business.

Sharjah is particularly active in promoting tourism. Already there are three tour operators in Sharjah. The first tourists arrived on charter flights from West Germany and Austria, and many are now returning for a second holiday. All three tour

Watching a camel race. For Sheikh and Bedouin alike, camels and camel racing are a part of the Arab way of life

operators offer trips around the other Emirates, as well as desert safaris with overnight camps and barbecues. Tourists can drive through *wadis*, across mountains and dunes, visit archaeological sites, museums and forts, see camels and camel races, date gardens and oases, meet Bedouin in the desert, wander round fascinating *souks* and pass beautiful mosques and palaces and picturesque old villages. They can experience for themselves the traditional hospitality of the UAE, exemplified in the age-old greeting: *Ahlan wa-sahlan* (''Hello—Welcome'').

Index

95

Heterick Memorial Library
Ohio Northern University

DUE	RETURNED	DUE	RETURNED
1. 2-18-97 FEB 1 8 1997		13.	
2. FEB 15 2007 5 2007		14.	
3. NOV 04 2007 NOV - 6 2007		15.	
4.		16.	
5.		17.	
6.		18.	
7.		19.	
8.		20.	
9.		21.	
10.		22.	
11.		23.	
12.		24.